C000132119

PALEO RECIPES FOR BUSY PEOPLE

QUICK AND EASY BREAKFAST, LUNCH, DINNER & DESSERTS RECIPE BOOK

By Jane Burton

JANE BURTON

- Visit the Author's Page -

www.amazon.com/author/janeburton

ISBN-13: 978-0992543525

ISBN-10: 0992543525

© 2014 by Jane Burton

Published by Kangaroo Flat Books

TABLE OF CONTENTS

WHAT IS THE PALEO DIET?

Why Paleo?

The Paleo diet is the only eating plan that works with you genetically as it assists you to become and remain energetic, lean and strong; in plain and simple English – really healthy! Based on research in biochemistry, biology, dermatology, Ophthalmology and numerous other discipline; it's our modern diet consisting primarily of processed foods, harmful trans fats and enormous amounts of sugar that's at the root of recent degenerative disease epidemics like Alzheimer's, diabetes, cancer, depression, heart disease, infertility, obesity and such.

WHAT YOU CAN EAT AND WHAT YOU CAN'T

Reality and being sensible is the Paleo Diet. The goal is to remove preservatives and additives from your diet and eat foods straight from nature. In its basic form, this is it in a nutshell. Think healthy, unprocessed or "unadulterated" foods as a Naturopath once told me! Think chemical free, natural, organic, home grown.

With only a few exceptions, this is the general rule.
· Fruits, veggies, lean meats, seafood, nuts & seeds and healthy fats are in –
· Whilst dairy, grains, processed foods, sugars, legumes, starches and alcohol are not allowed!

Now there are some grey areas in this diet and depending on how strict you are, some things are said to be allowed by some, while not others. A classic example of this is tomatoes and beans. Some say you can eat them and say you can't. If in doubt, use some common sense. If we can eat a vegetable raw, then surely the harmful chemicals can't be bad for these "controversial" foods in moderation only. After all the Paleo diet was based around a "caveman diet" which didn't include many of our modern day foods anyway. Another thing is that we encourage eating lean meats for good health, and this surely wasn't the case in the caveman days.

Olive oil is Paleo, so why not olives? It's all to do with preservatives and additives like many pickles, sausages and sauces on the market. If you do some searching, you may find some naturally preserved olives, which then leaves them perfectly Paleo! It really depends to what extent you are willing to take the most radical views. Make your own mind up.

If we take a sensible and realistic approach we won't beat ourselves up or lose faith in the diet because we ate some beans or oats 1 meal this week. **You are to be commended for making a positive change in your general eating habits.**

If you get stuck, grab my super quick *Paleo Food List* book for an easy guide as you shop for foods at the supermarket.

Building a Healthy Paleo Diet

Fruits and vegetables, being rich in antioxidants, minerals, nutrients and vitamins can minimize the risk of developing several common degenerative diseases including cancer, diabetes and general neurological decline.

Some vegetables are on the edge of being Paleo but sometimes common sense should prevail if they are beneficial in your diet. For example - are peas allowed in a Paleo diet? Well although they aren't supposed to be, a guide for me if a food is Paleo or not is whether it can be eaten raw or whether it needs to be cooked. Peas including snow peas and sugar snap can certainly be eaten raw. In my case freshly picked off the pea vine in my front yard on many occasions throughout the year. For those of you looking for a crunchy Paleo snack, I suggest there is nothing wrong with eating them in moderation. Actually moderation is the key.

The Paleo diet suggests we don't eat legumes. This is because legumes contain certain anti-nutrients like phytic acid and lectins. Phytic acid binds to the minerals magnesium, calcium, zinc, and iron in your gut and removes them, unabsorbed, from your body. And lectins aren't good for our stomach. However, a little occasionally isn't going to do much harm unless there is a reason you want to strictly adhere to the diet. This is where it can get confusing because nuts and seeds also contain these things, but they are allowed for anyone following the Paleo diet. I think this gets back to the quantity thing. Another common example many of us use when eating Paleo food is green beans and snow peas. These things also contain anti-nutrients, but if you're not eating loads of them then it's okay.If you are trying to add some liquid stock into your meals for the health benefits and flavor, then bone broth or stock is high in a very usable form of calcium, magnesium, silicon, sulphur and phosphorous plus many other trace nutrients. I often cook up chicken stock by adding the whole chicken (sometimes home grown) a few carrots, parsnip or swede, onion, celery and seasoning into a stock pot to boil. The taste is amazing in the soups, stews and casseroles. Very healthy indeed!

PROTEINS, FATS & THE PALEO LIFESTYLE

Lean Proteins not only help keep you feeling full between meals but also aid healthy bones, boost strong muscles and support optimal immune function.

Healthy Fats: Scientific studies reveal that illnesses like cancer, cognitive decline, diabetes, obesity and heart disease can be avoided through a diet rich in Monounsaturated and Omega-3 fats (healthy fats). These healthy type fats are found in avocados, grass fed meats, nuts, olive oil, fish oil and seeds.

Health Benefits of a Paleo Lifestyle: Typically these include anti-inflammatory, balanced energy throughout the day, burn off stored fat, clear skin & better teeth, improved sleep patterns, more efficient workouts, reduced allergies and stable blood sugar.

The Paleo diet works magic for weight loss and keeping your metabolism and energy levels charged.

THE PALEO DIET FOR WEIGHT LOSS

So many fad diets come and go over the years promising big results in weight loss but delivering very little. Most eventually crash or cause a barrage of shocking side effects including agonizing cravings, depleted energy levels and excruciating headaches just to name a few of the most common ones. **The Paleo Diet isn't really a diet as such since it's more of a 'as nature intended' healthy natural foods lifestyle choice.**

Men and women that have implemented and then followed the Paleo Lifestyle diet have all reported similar results; namely that it's a very simple concept once you get it and then it's easy to maintain. Perhaps it should be renamed 'Natural Human Diet' as it's really not rocket science but merely an approach in which unprocessed wholesome foods are consumed instead of unnatural refined or processed options that prevail nowadays.

WHAT'S THE CATCH?

Seriously there is none, although when first starting the Paleo Diet it's important not to go overboard and begin over eating. Sure the foods are natural and therefore 'healthy' but if you over do the calories even on healthy foods; you'll put on excess kilos instead of taking them off. You can learn more about the *Paleo Diet* in my book.

Like everything new, it's best to start slowly and to also do adequate research into the various Paleo diet foods, recipes and general rules. It may take a while to stock your pantry. Relax though; as it's definitely very easy to understand basic Paleo concepts like eating when hungry and stopping when full with no need to count calories or weigh food. These ideas are quite different to other diet plans that usually fail due to the fact that dieters often feel so bogged down with having to plan, weigh and stick to 4-6 balanced food pyramid meals. The Paleo diet lets you ditch both the tedious diet philosophy and time consuming process once and for all making life much more enjoyable! By eating natural unprocessed foods your overall health will improve, you'll reduce weight and generally feel better. Way to go!

Paleo Recipe Ideas for Busy People

Check out these terrific Paleo ideas that make great for healthy snacking, breakfasts or even a quick nutritious brunch or lunch. No specific recipe directions for these; as most are very easy to create by adapting regular non-paleo recipe favorites or need no preparation at all!

If you are ready to begin stocking the pantry with the basic Paleo foods but are standing in the supermarket and don't know which foods to buy, my *Paleo Shopping List* will help guide you through the aisles more quickly!

These ideas are perfect for busy people who want some quick, flexible ideas for eating Paleo.

· Sliced lean roast beef, fresh apricots or other seasonal fruit

· Apple slices & raw walnuts

· Egg Muffins: Easy to make in a big batch using a few favourite veggies & lean meat. Ready to enjoy whenever you feel like it!

· How about a Paleo trail mix made up of your very favourite nuts & dried fruit?

· Easy avocado – Simply cut in half & add a spoon!

· Banana bread made with almond meal & bananas!

· A Paleo platter: Selection of fresh fruits, cold unprocessed cuts of meats, baked veggies and sundried tomatoes!

· Tasty sweet berry muffins – Combine & bake eggs, coconut flour, nuts & berries

· A nice easy fresh fruit salad (whipped coconut cream is optional!)

· What about warm fruit custard made with eggs & coconut milk, nutmeg, cinnamon, berries, nuts & a banana?

· A enjoy a banana or anti-oxidant berry smoothie made with icy-cold coconut milk!

Canned sardines in olive oil (or spring water) served with a green salad and onion is always a good stand by if the fridge is bare!

Let's get cooking!

Paleo Breakfast Recipes

Paleo Breakfasts can be very traditional because eggs and bacon are in and so are healthy smoothies. My favorites!
With many store bought cereals off the morning menu exactly what do Paleo dieters usually eat for breakfast? You can get more breakfast ideas including Grain Free Granola in my *Paleo Cookbook*. If you're feeling particularly ravenous a serve of delicious chicken or turkey omelette should hit the spot. Or a quick nutritious breakfast smoothie may be ideal if you need something super easy to prepare and quick to guzzle down when you're on the go! Busy people with busy lives need to top up with super foods to keep those energy levels buzzing along. Here are some of my favorites!

Paleo Omelette

*All up it takes 15 minutes to have this lovely breakfast on the table.

Ingredients:

· 4 Free Range or Omega-3 eggs. Farm fresh even better!
· 1 Tbsp extra virgin olive oil
· 1 tsp fresh basil, finely chopped (optional) Use fresh herbs you like.
· 1/2 an avocado - sliced
· Fresh green salad (salad, sprouts, etc)
· Freshly ground black pepper
- Celery stick

Directions:

Whisk eggs till foamy in a small mixing bowl. Heat olive oil in a small frypan over medium heat adding eggs allowing them to cook for a few minutes. Sprinkle with basil and pepper. You can add chopped spinach to this recipe for some extra nutrition. Just fold in half way through continuing to cook until done). Garnish with sliced avocado and sliced celery. (I like celery in summer)

GRILLED GARLIC, MUSHROOMS & CHOPPED BACON

If you like your bacon super crispy, just cook it and the onions for 5 minutes before adding the other ingredients.

Ingredients:

. 1/2 onion, diced
· 2 cups sliced mushrooms (sliced). Add more if you like them lots!
· 1 cup of fresh, roughly chopped tomatoes (optional) If you are a strict Paleo then tomato may be out. I use it because I grow it in my back yard. It's organic and tastes amazing.
· 3 Tbsp English parsley finely chopped.
. 1/2 red capsicum finely chopped (optional)
· 3Tbsp extra virgin olive oil
· 3 garlic cloves (finely chopped or minced)
· Salt & Pepper to taste.

Directions:

Place all ingredients into a bowl and combine well. Fry over a medium-high heat, cooking for 5-8 minutes until bacon is crispy and the veggies are cooked through (even looking a little shrivelled up). Add salt & pepper to taste. Quick, tasty and easy for sure.
*You may like to serve this separately or on top of scrambled eggs.

PALEO ALMOND PANCAKES

Ingredients:

.2 eggs
.1 Tbsp vanilla extract
.½ cup unsweetened apple sauce or stewed apples, home made if you
have them.
.1½ cups almond flour
.½ tsp sea salt
.½ tsp baking soda
.strawberries for garnish

Directions:

Beat the eggs; mix in remaining ingredients except the almond flour,
mixing till smooth. Add flour; stirring to combine. Gently fry batter by
the spoonful in greased frypan; flipping to cook other side when
bubbles appear.
*Serve topped with fresh strawberries or whatever fresh fruits you like
best!

Banana, Berry & Acai Smoothie

Ingredients:

.1 - 2 large cold or frozen bananas
.1 cup coconut milk
.1 cup frozen or cold blueberries
.1 cup frozen or cold strawberries
.3/4 cup Acai juice (optional) Can use favorite fruit juice if prefer.

Directions:

Place all in a blender and mix until smooth. Fruits are flexible; If you have more of one, that's okay. It will still taste yummy!

STIR FRIED KALE & PORK BACON STRIPS

Ingredients:

· 1 bunch of kale thinly chopped
· 3 slices of finely sliced bacon or pork strips
· splash of Banyuls or Balsamic vinegar
· Kosher salt
· Freshly ground black pepper
. Finely sliced red chilli (optional)

Directions:

Gently fry the bacon strips and stir in the chopped Kale. Can remove leaves if prefer. Add other ingredients and serve immediately. Very flexible with the greens you add.

You may also like to take a look at the recipes in my *Kale Recipe Book*. It's loaded full of sides and kale meals!

PALEO SOUP RECIPES

Paleo Soups are a wonderful way to fill up with hearty, filling food that is great for weight loss and general health. Paleo soup recipes can be flexible and easily adapted to include ingredients you have in the pantry or fridge. It's easy to throw in some fresh vegetables you have on hand. Slow cooking soups are great for busy people getting home from work tired and not wanting to cook. Preparation times and clean up can be minimal too for recipes during the week. Eating Paleo is all about good health and nutrition, so adding some of your favorite vegetables, especially if they are home grown gives an additional energy boost.

If possible, make your own stock to add to your soups as this is high in calcium and other beneficial nutrients.

This is where the freezer can be your friend. Freeze the leftovers and have a meal prepared when you need it. Great for the busy lifestyle!

Curried Cream of Broccoli Soup

Ingredients:

· 750g (26oz) broccoli florettes
· 4 leeks
· 1 large brown onion
· 3 medium shallots or spring onions
· ¼ Jonathan apple (diced)
· 2 Tbsp olive oil
· 1L chicken stock
· 1 Tbsp curry powder (mild or hot)
· Salt to taste
· 1 cup coconut milk or cream

Directions:

Cut the entire broccoli into medium sized pieces. Roughly chop leeks, onion & shallots or spring onions. Dice the apple.
Heat oil in large pot; add prepped onions and sauté till soft (approx. 5-10 mins)
Add the broccoli & apple – stir well. Add chicken stock. Add enough to cover vegetables. Bring to boil and then turn heat down and simmer for about 20 minutes.
Add curry powder and seasonings to taste. Cool slightly and then blend in food processor or with a hand-held stick blender.
Add the coconut milk or cream, stirring well to combine.
Turn the heat back up and bring to boil again. Serve immediately.

Thai Chicken Curry Favorite

Either green curry paste or red curry paste works well in this recipe. Buy the curry paste in your local supermarket.

Ingredients:

.1lb (500g) of meat, cubed into bite sized pieces. I use beef or chicken.
.1 Tbsp olive oil or coconut oil
.2 cloves of chopped garlic
.1 inch cube of fresh minced ginger (optional)
.2 Kaffir lime leaves. I add lime leaves picked straight from my tree on the patio.
.1 Tbsp Green Curry Paste (or less for milder curry)
.1lb (500g) of vegetables. Choose sturdy varieties such as broccoli, peppers, and squashes. even asparagus. .Bamboo shoots, canned (optional)
.1 cup of coconut milk
.1/2 cup of stock (optional)
.Basil leaves or coriander leaves for garnish

Directions:

Slice your vegetables into manageable sizes. Prepare the meat by cutting into cubes or strips. Heat the pan to medium, then throw in the olive oil all the veggies and cook for a few minutes. Now put in the curry paste, minced or chopped garlic, minced ginger and stir until aromatic, about 2 mins. Now throw in the lime leaves and the cubed meat tossing as you go. Add coconut milk and stock and simmer for about 20 minutes (more for beef) until done. I add fresh herbs from the garden. Basil or coriander depending on my mood! Top with a slither of chili. This is a favorite at our house. The ginger, garlic and lime leaves can be blended and added together if you prefer.

My Beef Goulash Soup

My husband is Hungarian. This is a slight variation on the traditional Hungarian Beef Goulash recipe which originated in that country. It is quite flexible because some ingredients are optional, but not compromising taste like potato, stock and chili. Mind you...I think it tastes nicer with all these added. Sometimes I use potato, sometimes not.

This is a hearty Hungarian delight, and surprisingly very easy to make! It's more like a stew really. You will need a heavy pot (cast iron is good) with a lid.

Ingredients:

.1 Kg. (500g) lean cubed beef (I use gravy beef, chin beef or topside)
.1 Tbsp olive oil
.1 large onion
.1 heaped Tbsp Hungarian paprika
.1 tspn caraway seed water
.1/2 tspn marjoram or oregano
.Salt and black pepper to taste
.1 cup of water
.1 cup of beef stock (optional)
.1 seeded and cubed red pepper (capsicum)
.1/2 chili seeded and finely sliced

.1 small tin or a few fresh tomatoes
.1 bay leaf
.3 large potatoes, cubed (for strict paleos, use carrot or sweet potato)
.Approx.1 cup additional water

Directions:

In a heavy pot, fry the onion gently in the oil until golden (about 5 mins.) Add the paprika and stir in quickly, but immediately add in the cubed beef still stirring, working quickly not to burn the paprika (this can make the soup taste bitter) Now add 1/2 cup of water while stirring. Put the lid on and simmer. Meanwhile place caraway seeds in about 1/2 cup of water and microwave on a medium heat for about 30 seconds to heat. Now strain and place the caraway water into the pot. Add herbs, bay leaf, seasoning, capsicum, tomatoes and chili. Cook over low simmering heat for about 1 hour. When meat is almost done, add cubed potatoes. Cook for further 30 - 40 mins until done. Serve with a sprinkle of herbs on top. Absolutely yummy! This Paleo recipe can be cooked in a slow cooker.

ROASTED PUMPKIN SOUP

Ingredients:

· 2kg (4 1/2 pounds) approximately of pumpkin
· 2 Tbsp olive oil
· 4 cups home made chicken stock with bone
· 1 1/2 cups water
· Salt and ground black pepper
· ½ tsp onion or garlic flakes
· 1 tsp dried tarragon leaves
. pinch of curry powder (optional)

Directions:

Prepare pumpkin by cutting in half and removing the seeds. Brush with oil; placing onto baking sheet in hot oven (350F); cut side facing down and bake for about 1 hour or until done.
When cooked, scoop out pumpkin flesh with a spoon and place into a large cooking pot. Add stock and water;. Add garlic flakes, tarragon leaves, curry powder and seasonings, mix well with hand held stick blender until smooth.

Place pot on a medium to high heat and bring to the boil. Reduce heat to very low and simmer for about 1 hour; stirring occasionally.
*Serves 8-10. Swirl a small amount of coconut cream on top.

I often don't use the blender until the end of cooking, then serve immediately.

PALEO GROUND BEEF AND VEGETABLE SLOW COOKER SOUP

Ingredients:

· 500g (just over 1 pound) lean minced beef
· 1 medium brown onion (chopped)
· 2 cups fresh mixed vegetables such as snow peas and carrots. (Frozen okay too)
· 2 large tins of tomatoes, or 5 fresh home grown.
· 2 cups water
· Salt, garlic flakes and ground black pepper to taste

Directions:

Brown minced beef & onion in frypan; drain off any liquid and transfer to large pot or slow cooker. Add remaining ingredients; cover and cook for 4 hours on low setting or simmer on stove top for about an hour. This is a great recipe for kids learning to cook.
*Too easy but very tasty! Feel free to add a little heat with some hot peppers and warm spices or go more Italian with some oregano or basil. I did sneak some green beans in from the garden. The kids love them...I'm not going to argue!

CHICKEN PALEO RECIPES

Chicken Paleo Dinners

Chicken is undoubtedly one of the most versatile meats, is quick to cook and also tastes great; so it makes good sense to include some delicious Paleo poultry main meals! Chicken is not only cheap, but also quick and easy for beginners starting out learning to cook. Be aware of clean knives and working surfaces to avoid cross contamination.

Let's take a look at some easy Paleo chicken dishes for when you are in a hurry to get food on the table.

PALEO CHICKEN BREAST TERIYAKI WITH PINEAPPLE

*This is a chicken recipe with a Japanese twist.

Ingredients:

· 1 Tbsp coconut/olive oil
· 500g (just over 1 pound) chicken breasts (skinless)
· ¼ tsp sea salt
· ¼ tsp ground black pepper
· 1 onion (diced)
· 1 red capsicum (diced)
· Coconut aminos . This is a substitute for soy sauce
· 1 cup diced pineapple
· beans for non strict paleo (optional) I had my own fresh home grown beans. Broccoli or cauliflower is good too.
· 3 small cos lettuce hearts if you have them.

Directions:

Chop the chicken into small 1in pieces, seasoning with salt & pepper. Heat the oil in large frypan. Add chicken and onions; frying over med-high heat. Cook about 5 minutes.
Add about 2Tbsp coconut aminos (or use soy sauce); cooking for another 5 minutes. Add prepared pineapple and red capsicum. Cook until chicken is completely cooked through and veggies are tender. Serve over chopped cos lettuce.

CHICKEN THIGHS WITH BACON

Ingredients:

· 1kg chicken thigh fillets or breasts
· 125g (4 1/2oz) lean bacon strips (diced)
· 1 of home made chicken stock (on bone)
. Fresh herbs you prefer can be added.

Directions:

Fry diced bacon in hot frypan with a little olive oil. Remove from pan. Now place chicken into the frypan and cook in the bacon fat / juices over medium heat for about 10 minutes until the chicken is browned well all over. Remove any excess fat from the pan with a spoon. Pour in the stock. Bring to boil; then reduce to low heat and cover with lid. Simmer for 30 minutes and add the bacon back into pan.
* This is one of the simplest chicken dinner recipes to prepare. Scrumptiously divine! Serve with salad and/or veggies.

DELICIOUS BUTTER CHICKEN RECIPE

Ingredients:

· 2 x 2 Tbsp of grass-fed butter or olive oil
· 1kg chicken thigh / breast fillets (cut into chunk sized pieces)
· 2 tsp garam masala (optional)
· 2 tsp Hungarian paprika
· 2 tsp ground coriander
· 1 1/2 tbsp finely grated fresh ginger (I use the small blender for this)
· 1/4 tsp chili powder (to your taste)
· a sprig of basil or coriander for garnish.
· 1 can of tomato puree (or use fresh)
· 1 - 1 1/2 cups coconut milk (or coconut cream)
· 1 Tbsp lemon juice

Directions:

Fry chopped chicken in melted butter or oil (olive oil) in a medium to hot frypan. This may need to be done in 2 batches using extra butter / oil as required. Remove chicken from pan when totally cooked. Add the 2nd lot of butter / oil to pan, add spices and cook for 2-3 minutes or till you smell the aroma! Place chicken back into pan; coating and mixing in with the spiced butter. Add tomatoes and simmer about 15 minutes, stirring occasionally.

Add coconut milk & lemon juice; simmering for about more 5 minutes. Garnish with fresh herbs, I've used coriander. I grow it and absolutely adore it. Peppery basil is another of my favorites.
*Enjoy this tasty Indian delight known as Murg Makhani without feeling guilty! This recipe may seem to have a lot of ingredients for beginners, but it's actually very easy to make. Give it a try. We love it in our house.

FISH DINNER RECIPES

As we know fish is a great source of Omega 3 and healthy oils for our body in general including our heart, cholesterol level, skin and hair. Many people the world over take Omega supplements and Fish oil vitamins daily to improve their health, including joint pain and arthritis.

The other benefit of course is that fish tastes wonderfully light and is a special treat, especially in the warmer months. We should try to include fish in our diets at least once a week. Here are a few recipes other than the delicious and simple grilled fish with herbs and lemon which is a good old stand-by in our house when we are in a hurry.

ASIAN PEPPER SHRIMP

Ingredients:

.3 Tbsp coconut oil
.4 cloves garlic (minced)
.750g (25oz) raw prawns (peeled with tails intact)
.1 Tbsp Coconut aminos (soy sauce substitute)
.1 Tbsp fish sauce
.1 tsp black pepper (or to taste)
.¼ cup chopped fresh cilantro

Directions:

Melt coconut oil over low heat in large frypan. Add minced garlic, stir for 2-3 minutes being careful not to brown it. Add prawns and sauté about 5 minutes till cooked through (pinkish). Add coconut aminos, fish sauce & pepper; sautéing for 1-2 minutes more.

Remove prawns and plate up. Quickly boil combined liquid and oil in frypan; then reduce and cook contents down. Pour over prawns to serve. Top each with sprinkling of chopped cilantro to serve. *Serves 4

CRUMBED CASHEW FISH

Ingredients:

· 400g (14oz) white fish (cut into palm sized pieces)
· 2 tsp coriander
· 2 tsp cumin
· 2 tsp black peppercorns
· 2 tsp black mustard seed
· 3 tbsp cashew nut flour
· A pinch cayenne pepper (optional)
· A handful of crushed cashews
· 1 onion peeled & finely chopped
· Olive oil
· A handful of fresh coriander or parsley

Directions:

Grind black peppercorns & mustard seed with mortar & pestle.
Combine ground pepper, mustard, cumin, coriander & cayenne in a
bowl. Add cashew flour.
Heat a frypan to high, dry fry crushed cashews till golden and then set
aside. Add small amount of oil to pan; sauté onions for 5 minutes and
then set aside with cashews.
Add enough oil to frypan to shallow fry fish which has been
generously coated with cashew and spice mix. Fish should only need
about 2-3 minutes each side. Fry till crisp and golden!
Return onions and cashews to frypan for 1- 2 minutes adding
seasoning. Serve with fresh coriander.
*This dish is not only quick, easy and good for you- but it's also
bursting with lots of flavour. It's perfect for the whole family!

SALMON WITH MANGO RECIPE

Salmon is absolutely delicious and although quite expensive, you need very little to fill the tummy! I've included this recipe because it's super quick, easy and super tasty! Small salmon steaks can be cooked on a high heat with the skin on and cooked with a crispy grilled crust on the outside. Some prefer it just cooked through.

Ingredients:

· 500g (just over 1 pound) salmon fillet
· Salt & pepper to taste
· 1 medium lemon (sliced)
· 1 mango (peeled & chopped)
· 1 Tbsp olive oil

Directions:

Place salmon (skin side down) on baking sheet
Season salmon with salt & pepper to taste
Place sliced lemons & chopped mangoes over salmon
Dash lightly with olive oil
Cover; placing in fridge for 1- 2 hours
Bake salmon in medium oven for 12-15 minutes. *Serves 4
*Nice & easy marinated salmon with fresh mangoes and lemon. Serve with fresh steamed vegetables and/or a salad.

BEEF PALEO DINNERS

Although we know that caveman ate meat, they probably ate **loads of fat with it for much needed energy.** However march on through time and today most of us don't require those extra calories and fat in our diets. We understand that too much animal fat is not good for our cholesterol levels. For this reason it's best to eat lean meats when eating a Paleo diet. Following are some of our favorite quick beef dinner ideas.

Check out more of my Paleo Lunch and Dinner Recipes on Amazon.

Almond Flour Recipes

Coconut Milk Recipes

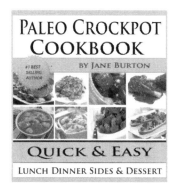

Crockpot Recipes

BEEF SALSA VERDE

Ingredients:

· 1 sliced tomato
· ½ cup parsley leaves
· ½ cup basil leaves
· 2 cloves garlic
· 2 Tbsp capers (drained)
· 1 anchovy fillet (cut into pieces)
· 1 cup extra virgin olive oil
· 2 tablespoons fresh lime juice
· Salt & pepper (to taste)
· 750g (about 25oz) lean sirloin/ fillet steak or similar piece of roasting beef
· 5 cups baby field greens
.Sprinkle with fresh rosemary

Directions:

Purée parsley, basil, garlic, capers, tomato & anchovy fillet in blender; slowly add olive oil until combined. Add lime juice, salt & pepper blending till well combined and smooth. Adjust seasonings to taste and set sauce aside.

Season and grill or panfry steak to your particular preference. When cooked; slice thinly and drizzle with salsa verde. Garnish with some rosemary sprigs or herbs of your choice. True caveman diet food!

BEEF & VEGETABLE STEW

We love stews in the colder months. Great as a slow cooker recipe for busy people coming home from work or on the stove top.

Ingredients:

·1 - 1 1/2 pounds stewing or gravy beef. Cut off excess fat.
·4 cups beef stock (homemade if possible)
·1 1/2 tbsp olive oil
·1 cup chopped brown onion
·3 large carrots, peeled and chopped;
·2 potatoes, peeled and cubed (optional)
·1 celery stick, chopped
·1 can diced tomatoes
·1 bay leaf
·1 small sprig of fresh rosemary, finely chopped
·½ tsp fresh thyme, finely chopped
·1/4 tspn chili powder (optional)
· (I add Zucchini if it's in season)
·Salt & black pepper to taste

Directions:

In a large heavy bottom pot of saucepan over a medium to high heat, combine the onions, celery, carrots, potatoes, if using, as well as the olive oil. Cook for about 4 minutes, stirring constantly.
Turn heat to high and add the beef to the saucepan, followed by the tomatoes, beef stock, rosemary and thyme. Add chili to taste with salt and pepper. Reduce heat once boiling. Cover the saucepan and cook for about 1 - 1 1/2 hours, allowing the stew to simmer and get that rich full flavor. Stir occasionally. Depending on how much liquid you want, you can remove the lid and cook uncovered for about 45 minutes to reduce. If the stew is too thick, then add a little more stock or water.

FAVORITE PRIME RIB ROAST

Ingredients:

· 3 tsp fresh ginger (grated)
· ½ cup orange marmalade (unprocessed)
· 8 cloves garlic (minced)
· 1 Tbsp mustard powder
· 2kg (4 1/2 pounds) roasting beef (Sirloin, Topside, Scotch)
· ¼ cup olive oil
· Freshly ground black pepper (to taste)

Directions:

For the marinade: Mix together ginger, marmalade, mustard and ½ the garlic
Prick holes all over meat with a fork and place slithers of garlic (remaining 4 cloves) inside holes. Pour marinade over beef; cover and refrigerate for 2 hours or more. Baste occasionally.
Preheat oven to 200C. pour olive oil over beef, season with pepper and bake for and then cook it for 1 hour covered with aluminium foil.
Remove foil after 1 hour, baste and reduce oven to 165C and continue roasting till cooked to your liking. Allow roast to rest for about 30 minutes before slicing. I added some fresh mashed potato and parsnip from the garden.

Paleo Chili Beef for Kids

When the kids need something hearty in their bellies; try some Paleo Chili as it's guaranteed to satisfy! *This recipe is a favorite with my Paleo cave-kids!

Ingredients:

· 2 Tbsp coconut oil
· 1 diced onion
· 6 stalks of celery (diced)
· 4 garlic cloves (minced)
· 3 1/2 pounds (about 1.3kg) ground beef
· 4 tsp cumin
· 4 tsp chilli powder
· 4 tsp oregano
· 2 x 12 oz jars of medium to hot salsa
· 2 x 8 oz cans of diced tomatoes
· 2 x 7 oz cans of green chillies
· 4 tsp sea salt

Directions:

Using a large pot; fry onions, celery & garlic in coconut oil over med-high heat. Cook for about 4 minutes adding beef and spices. Cook for further 5 minutes; stirring constantly. Add tomatoes, salsa green chillies & salt. Simmer for about 1 hour. *Serves a hungry family of 4 - 6 Great when you are in need of a quick and easy recipe. I like to add a small bunch of chopped parsley at the end of cooking.

Pork Paleo Dinners

Pork is another popular meat for eating Paleo at it's best. As with beef and chicken, pork can be very flexible with what vegetables you cook to accompany it. Many different cuts of pork can be used, again try to keep it lean, or at least cut off excess fat before eating. It is scrumptious fried or grilled. I love it in stir frys. Bacon used in its various methods for cooking is always a big hit.

Beware "made up blends" of meats. When shopping I ask myself (or the butcher) "would this likely be processed with other things added, or natural"

SPICY BREADED PORK CHOPS

Ingredients:

· 2 tsp cayenne pepper(use less if too hot)
· 3 Tbsp coconut oil (divided)
· 1½ cups almond flour
· 4 large lean pork chops

Directions:

Mix cayenne pepper & 2 Tbsp coconut oil in a bowl. Coat both sides of pork chops.
Cover both sides of pork chops with almond flour until fully enclosed. Heat 1 Tbsp coconut oil in frypan over a medium heat. Add chops when pan is hot; cooking on both sides till cooked through.

*You may like to cut back on the cayenne and lower the cooking temperature also if kitchen is not well ventilated as things can get rather smoky! Or better still grill the pork chops on a bar-b-q! One thing for sure is that these chops are really tasty & filling!

ROASTED GARLIC & HERB CRUSTED PORK ROAST

Ingredients:

· 2-3kg (about 4 1/2 pounds) Pork Loin Roast
· 2 Bulbs Roasted Garlic
· 1 Tbsp fresh sage (chopped)
· 1½ Tbsp fresh rosemary (chopped)
· 1½ Tbsp fresh thyme (chopped)
· Salt & Pepper (to taste)

Directions:

Preheat oven to 475 F
To make the rub – Place chopped sage, rosemary & thyme in bowl.
Add salt & pepper.
Prepare pork loin – Trim fat from pork. Season with salt & pepper.
Rub pork with mashed roasted garlic & mixed chopped herbs evenly
over roast.
Place in prepared roasting pan with capsicum or favorite vegetables.
Roast pork in a hot oven (475F) for 30 minutes; and then reduce to
425F roasting for an additional hour. Let it sit for around 20 minutes
before carving as it will continue cooking while it rests. *Serves 6+

*Serve as a traditional roast with roasted pumpkin, potatoes, carrots &
asparagus. Then re-purpose for another delicious Paleo dinner by

topping a fresh green salad with thinly sliced left over pork and roasted sweet potato chunks! Delicious!

MUM'S PORK CHOPS

Ingredients:

· 4 lean pork chops
· Salt & pepper (to taste)
· ½ cup Dijon mustard
· 1 tsp mustard powder
· 1 tsp dried thyme
· 1 tsp garlic (minced)
· 1 Tbsp coconut oil

Directions:

Preheat oven to 425 F
Season pork chops with salt & pepper. Combine mustard, mustard powder, thyme & garlic in a small bowl. Mix well. Spread evenly over both sides of pork chops.
Heat oil in a large frypan over medium-high, add chops and brown for about 2 minutes per side. Transfer chops to baking dish and cook in oven for another 5-8 minutes or until cooked through. Serve over sautéed baby spinach and/or a scrumptious fresh green salad. *Serves about 4.

PALEO SMOOTHIES

Paleo smoothies are quick and easy alternatives for breakfast, lunch or as a healthy in between Snack.

Paleo Diet Smoothies are perfect for those embracing a Paleo lifestyle because not only do smoothies offer muscle-building, fat burning, mood-enhancing & brain boosting benefits but these blender shakes are so easy to prepare. They taste awesome too! These are great for busy moms, dads and kids going to work or school. We love making smoothies in our family. I am also into healthy, nutrient rich juicing.

QUICK & EASY FRUIT SMOOTHIE

Ingredients:

· 1 cup apple juice (unsweetened)
· 1 frozen banana (peeled)
· ½ cup of frozen fruit (blueberries, blackberries, strawberries, melons, peaches, mango, etc)

Directions:

Pour apple juice into blender; add cut up banana and blend creamy. Add remaining fruit and blend. I love making smoothies...they are SO flexible. Almost any combination tastes amazing!

Mango & Kale Smoothie

Ingredients:

· 2 cups fresh kale (washed & in chunks. (sometimes I use steamed spinach instead)
. 1 1/2 mangoes
· juice from 1/2 a lime
· 1 kiwifruit (peeled & chopped)
· 1 1/2 cups chilled coconut milk (or coconut cream)

Directions:

Process all ingredients in a blender until well mixed. Simple, healthy and delicious. serve & enjoy!

STRAWBERRY COCONUT ALMOND SMOOTHIE

Ingredients:

· approx. 6-8 strawberries (sometimes I use fresh pears)
· kiwi fruit & strawberry for garnish
· 250ml coconut milk or unsweetened almond milk
· 1 tsp almond butter
· 1 tsp organic honey

Directions:

Simply place all ingredients in a blender and mix until smooth. Garnish with strawberries, kiwifruit or coconut shavings. Add a swizzle stick for fun!
*Serves 1-2

PALEO DESSERT RECIPES

Desserts are served after a meal or sometimes just as a **morning or afternoon tea "snack".** Desserts are delicious and fine in moderation. Remember balance in your diet is the key to being healthy and full of energy. Stay away from packaged foods and anything artificial. We need to substitute processed sugar. Stevia, coconut oil and quality maple syrup being common alternatives. Raw honey is popular - that means as it exists more naturally in the beehive where it is extracted without adding heat. A bit like cold pressed oils. Many smoothies are good of course because of the natural sugars. Substituting sugar for dates and other fruits is a favorite.

If you want to entertain people, or just treat yourself, **grab my free** *Paleo Desserts Book* here at *http://paleorecipeblog.com*
There is also a meal planner you can print off.

Go back to the old rule of the Paleo diet - no processed food. Keep the ingredients fresh and simple. Here are just a handful of recipe ideas for eating Paleo desserts. If we are in a hurry, fruit salad with a dob of coconut cream or a smoothie if a life saver!

Sweet Potato Ice cream

Ingredients:

· 1 baked or steamed medium sized Sweet Potato (remove skin)
· 1 can coconut milk or coconut cream
· 1 Tbsp maple syrup or honey
· 2 egg yolks
· 2 Tbsp cinnamon
· 1 tsp vanilla extract (essence is okay)
· Large pinch of nutmeg

Directions:

Put the ice cream mix in the ice cream machine in freezer overnight.
Place sweet potato & coconut milk in food processor; processing to a
pureed consistency.
Add all remaining ingredients and mix until well. Add a pinch of salt
(optional)

Place mixture into a bowl and chill in fridge for at least two hours.
Transfer mixture to ice cream maker and follow instructions, churning

for about 25-30 minutes. Pour into individual glasses is another option for a finished look and freeze.

Banana Coconut Paleo Muffins

Ingredients:

· 4 fresh eggs
· 4 bananas (must be very ripe)
· 1 tsp vanilla extract
· ¼ cup coconut butter or olive oil
· 5 Tbsp coconut flour
· ½ cup maple sugar (or raw honey)
· 1 tsp baking powder
· ¼ tsp cinnamon
· ¼ tsp salt
· Natural walnuts, almonds, pecans, macadamia or cashew nuts to garnish

Directions:

Heat the oven to 350 degrees and prepare a 12 muffin lined tin.
Mix dry ingredients in mixing bowl. Mash bananas in food processor. This doesn't need to be really smooth. Add coconut butter or olive oil

and blend together briefly. Add eggs & vanilla again blending only for about 10 seconds.

Add wet mixture to dry ingredients; mix gently with a spatula till combined. Don't over mix!

Divide mixture evenly between muffin liners with a spoon.

Top each muffin with walnuts or nuts of choice. Bake in a medium to hot oven for about 30 minutes.

*YUM!!!! The kids will absolutely love these! I find over mixing once the flour goes in can make muffins tough to eat.

Yummy Apple Pie Balls

These are perfect for kids lunch box treats or anytime treats for that matter! Can use stewed apple, but it must be a "dry" mix.

Ingredients:

· 1 cup cinnamon apple chips (store bought or homemade)
· 1 cup cinnamon apple rings
· 1 cup dried coconut flakes
· 1 cup soft dates
· ¾ cup raisins or sultanas

Directions:

Place everything except raisins in a food processor and process about 2 minutes or until mixture would form a ball if moulded in your hand. The apple chips should be 1/2 cm shards. Add raisins and blend (use pulse button) a few more times to get the correct consistency. If you prefer a smoother mix; simply process all ingredients together at start (including raisins).
Form into small sized balls. You may roll them in extra coconut flakes if dough is too sticky. (my kids were a little heavy on the coconut)
These are nice served with a scoop of the Sweet Potato Ice cream recipe.
*To make your own apple chips simply sprinkle thinly sliced cored apple rings with cinnamon and pop into low heat oven to dehydrate and crisp up. Once they've cooled, they're ready. Store or enjoy! * For store bought cinnamon chips; find a brand that contains apple, coconut oil & cinnamon. Read the food labels, think natural!

That ends this Paleo recipe book. Happy cooking and I hope you like these Paleo recipes as much as I do. You can check out some of my other books on my Author Page. If you have enjoyed this book, or would like to share a recipe, write a review below.

If you have a minute, please leave a review on Amazon, thanks!

Customer Reviews

218 Reviews

5 star:	(163)
4 star:	(22)
3 star:	(12)
2 star:	(9)
1 star:	(12)

Average Customer Review

★★★★½ (218 customer reviews)

Create your own review

PALEO RECIPE RESOURCES

*The Paleo Diet by Loren Cordain.
*Grain Brain by David Perlmutter
*Check out my other Paleo Recipe Books on Amazon which are all available on Kindle. They are all in full color and include links to useful information. All are free or at a special price on a regular basis.

MY FREE GIFT TO YOU

As a valued customer I wanted to send you a free gift :) It's my Paleo Desserts and Treats Recipe Book. You can download the book at the address below. I hope you enjoy it!

I'd appreciate you hitting the **"share"** or **"like"** button with your friends if you think they may like it too. Thanks!

http://paleorecipeblog.com

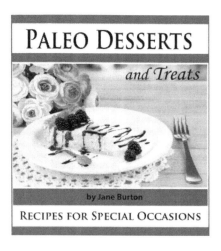

NOTES

COPYRIGHT

All Rights Reserved

Paleo Recipes: Copyright © 2014 by Jane Burton

Copyright: The author Jane Burton has exclusively published this book and holds all copyrights to it. A great deal of work has been put into producing it. No part of this publication may be reproduced, stored in retrieval system, copied in any form or by any means, electronic, mechanical, photocopying, recording or otherwise transmitted without written permission from the publisher. You must not circulate this book in any format unless asking first. Thank you for your honesty and understanding.

Disclaimer: This book is from my experiences eating and cooking using Paleo recipes. It has been prepared in good faith, with the goal being to share recipe favorites with others. I am not liable in any way how you choose to use this information as it is an account on my own experiences eating Paleo.

9562876R00039

Printed in Great Britain
by Amazon.co.uk, Ltd.,
Marston Gate.